TEACHING READING USING PICTURE BOOKS

2-3

Written by
Traci Ferguson Geiser

Editors: Carla Hamaguchi and Heather Butler
Illustrator: Jenny Campbell
Cover Illustrator: Rick Grayson
Designer/Production: Moonhee Pak/Cari Helstrom
Cover Designer: Barbara Peterson
Art Director: Tom Cochrane
Project Director: Carolea Williams

Table of Contents

Introduction

Picture books open the imagination. They excite and inspire children. What better way to illustrate key reading skills than through cherished picture books? These read-alouds engage children in learning how our language works. Research has shown that effective reading programs must include instruction in five areas: vocabulary, fluency, comprehension, phonics, and phonemic awareness. Phonemic awareness is mainly covered in kindergarten and first grade. The aim of this book is to use the friendly, engaging format of picture books to combine instruction in *vocabulary, fluency, comprehension,* and *phonics,* while also providing *writing activity reproducibles.* A summary of the four areas of instruction covered in this book follows.

There are two basic types of vocabulary: *receptive* (vocabulary a child understands when he or she hears it) and *expressive* (vocabulary a child uses when speaking). Both need to be developed for a child to read well. However, when studying how children acquire and use vocabulary, it's more helpful to think in terms of spoken and written vocabulary. Emerging readers lean heavily on their knowledge of spoken vocabulary to decode new words they encounter in text—whether or not they actually use those words in conversation. It is much more difficult for a child to decode a new word he or she has not heard. As children develop their reading skills, they also develop their written vocabulary. Children cannot understand texts that contain an unreasonable number of unfamiliar words. The following are six strategies to help increase children's receptive and expressive vocabulary:

- **Preteaching Vocabulary**—Before reading a story, teach children words that they may find difficult to read or understand. This should include words important to the story, words with multiple meanings or spellings, and words that are used in an uncommon manner.

- **Using Context Clues**—Children use illustrations, other words in the sentence, and surrounding sentences to decode an unknown word.
- **Repeated Exposure**—Children are introduced to a new word and are then given many situations to hear and use the word over time.
- **Extended Instruction**—Children are given extended instruction and activities to reinforce and practice the new words.
- **Using Reference Books**—Children are taught strategies to figure out the pronunciation and meaning of new words.
- **Using Word Parts**—Children take a word and break it into parts (e.g., prefixes, suffixes, compound words) to decipher meaning.

Fluency instruction may seem cosmetic on the surface. Its aim is to produce a reader who sounds natural while reading. Fluent readers are accurate, quick, and able to read with expression. They make the reading sound interesting. But beyond enhancing the experience for listeners, fluent readers are also demonstrating skills that are crucial to their understanding of what they read. Fluent readers recognize words at a glance, group words into meaningful phrases, and move beyond the struggle to decode individual words. They are able to focus on making sense of what they read.

Fluency is often the missing bridge between being able to "read" a text and being able to understand it. Readers who are decoding word-by-word sound plodding and choppy. And worse, they are too busy to have time to think about what they are reading as they read it. The most effective way to encourage fluency in children is to model it and to provide children with frequent opportunities to read aloud. Children who know you are listening for fluency are often motivated to read more fluently.

Direct instruction in comprehension helps children to understand what they read, to remember it, and to be able to communicate with others about what they read. Children who have a reason for reading a piece beyond its role as an assignment (e.g., I'm going to find out how bats see in the dark) are more likely to show a higher degree of comprehension when they have completed the reading. The process of comprehension is a complicated one. One of the most important aspects of comprehension is children's ability to know when they do not understand what they are reading. Good readers know when their own comprehension has broken down. Research has identified five effective techniques you can teach children in order to improve their comprehension skills:

- **Monitoring Comprehension**—Teach children to be aware of what they do and don't understand (metacognition) and to be willing to solve problems in comprehension as they occur.

- **Using Graphic Organizers**—Graphic organizers help children filter out the unimportant details and focus on the story structure and relationships. They also help children craft well-organized summaries.
- **Answering Questions**—Children answer the teacher's questions, both literal (facts explicitly stated in the text) and inferential (making connections or inferences).
- **Generating Questions**—Children generate questions about the text. Initially, they focus on literal or explicit questions. Over time, they will model their questions on the questions the teacher asks of them.
- **Summarizing**—Summarizing involves children processing the key points in the text and explaining those points in their own words.

Phonics connects the sounds of language to the written symbols that represent them. Phonics instruction helps children learn these relationships and begin to understand the alphabetic principle— the predictable patterns of written letters and spoken sounds. Phonics instruction must be systematic and explicit to be effective. That is, phonics instruction must follow a logical sequence that introduces the most common and simple relationships first and builds in complexity. It must be presented clearly and with specific, measurable objectives. Phonics instruction is not always intuitive. In addition, effective phonics instruction includes the opportunity, on an ongoing basis, for children to apply the new skills they're learning to words, sentences, and larger pieces of text.

How to Use This Book

This book is designed to provide teachers with an easy guide to cover four key areas of reading instruction, as well as written activities, while reading popular literature selections.

Skills Taught

This section (see pages 6–7) provides a list of the skills taught with each literature selection. This is a quick resource to find which lessons teach a specific skill. Refer to this list when your class needs added emphasis in one of these areas.

General Activity Ideas

This section (starting on page 8) includes activity ideas for the four key areas of reading instruction. These activities can be used with any literature selection. Choose one of these activities when children need a little more practice in a given area. These can be used in addition to the activities provided for each literature selection. Also included in this section are a Making Connections reproducible and a Character Map reproducible, as well as two lists of sample questions—Questions to Ask Readers and Questions Good Readers Ask.

Activities for Literature Selections

There are four reading skills activities to accompany each literature selection. Read aloud the literature selection. Then have children complete each activity. Depending on your class, you can spread the activities over the course of a week, do a couple of activities per day, or do all the activities in one day.

Writing Activity Reproducibles

For each literature selection, there is a writing activity reproducible to reinforce one of the other activities or to introduce a creative writing exercise. These pages can be reproduced and sent home for homework, or you can have children work on them independently in class.

Literature Selections

A list of the literature selections used in this book is provided on page 79 in a convenient reference format that includes authors and publishers.

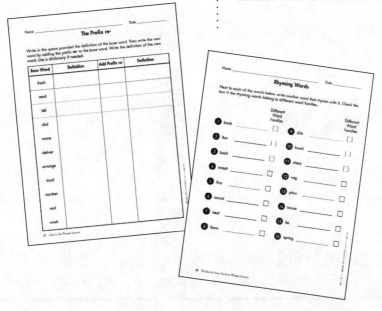

Skills Taught

	Vocabulary	Preteaching Vocabulary	Using Context Clues	Repeated Exposure	Extended Instruction	Using Reference Books	Using Word Parts	Fluency	Child-Adult Reading	Tape-Assisted Reading
Alexander and the Terrible, Horrible, No Good, Very Bad Day			•							
Caps for Sale							•			
Where the Wild Things Are						•			•	
Miss Spider's Tea Party				•						
The Little Old Lady Who Was Not Afraid of Anything					•					
A Turkey for Thanksgiving					•					
Thomas' Snowsuit						•				•
The Hat					•					
I Love You the Purplest							•		•	
The Valentine Bears				•						
Mama, Do You Love Me?		•								
Rumpelstiltskin		•								•
The Day the Goose Got Loose		•								
The Monkey and the Crocodile							•			
The Cat in the Hat		•								
Make Way for Ducklings			•						•	
McDuff Saves the Day						•				
Blueberries for Sal			•							•
Swimmy				•					•	

Choral Reading	Partner Reading	Reader's Theater	Comprehension	Monitoring Comprehension	Using Graphic Organizers	Answering Questions	Generating Questions	Summarizing	Phonics	Long and Short Vowels	Verb Suffixes	Vowel Diphthongs	The Sounds of oo	R-controlled Vowels	Consonant Blends	Consonant Digraphs	Contractions	Rhyming Words	Letter Combinations	The Sound of qu	The /s/ and /z/ Sounds
●					●												●				
●								●												●	
						●				o											
●						●				ea											
		●						●								wh					
		●		●									●								
				●							-ed										
		●				●	●												-dge		
				●											st						
	●					●								●							
	●				●					e											
								●													●
	●						●											●			
		●						●			-ing										
	●				●							ou/ow									
						●	●			u											
	●				●														-ould		
						●	●			i											
				●											sw						

General Activity Ideas

Children learn most of their vocabulary through indirect methods. They hear a given word over and over in different contexts. Initially, this builds recognition, and over time, it leads to a more complete understanding of the word's meaning. Only a small portion of a child's vocabulary is gained through direct instruction, but it is still an important part of vocabulary acquisition. When providing vocabulary instruction, be sure to focus on words that are important for understanding the text, words that are useful to know, and difficult words (e.g., long words, words with uncommon spellings or multiple or uncommon meanings, and idioms). Below are some vocabulary activity ideas.

Act It Out

Write a vocabulary word on the board, and read it aloud. If the word is a noun, use gestures to show the typical size and shape of the item. Pantomime how the item is used, showing how much effort it might take to use it, its relative weight, and expressions that show how enjoyable the experience is or is not. If the word is a verb, pantomiming action can provide children with a memorable level of understanding. Use pantomime to illustrate an adjective by showing how something is changed by it or responds to it. For example, you might demonstrate *blustery* by pantomiming trying to walk outside on a windy day, losing your hat, and leaning into the wind.

Use Words in Context

Challenge children to use a vocabulary word in context during the week after the word is introduced. Keep a tally of each time a child uses the word correctly. At the end of the week, count the tallies. If the class gets ten tally marks at the end of the week, every child receives a reward or prize.

Role-Play

List the vocabulary words on the board, and discuss their meanings with the class. Divide the class into small groups, and assign each group one of the vocabulary words. Ask each group to create a skit in which they use the word at least three times. Have one child in each group hold up a sign with the printed word each time the word is used in the skit.

Fluency

There are a number of strategies that can be applied in the classroom and at home to maximize opportunities for coaching readers as they read aloud. When you provide a child with fluency instruction and practice, reading material should be at his or her independent reading level. No more than 1 in 20 words should be unfamiliar. Some suggested methods are summarized below.

Model Fluent Reading

Read aloud to your class daily. Model expression and pacing as you read. Occasionally, stop and point out what you are doing and why. For example, you might say *Did you notice how my voice paused after the words* **tiny mouse**? (Point to the words.) *That is because there is a comma there, and a comma tells me to pause for a moment.*

Children Read Aloud Modeled Text

After you model how to read the text, provide repeated opportunities for children to read the same material. Children should reread a text at least four times to become fluent. Some experiences should be whole group and some should be individual. The following methods are five ways to provide children with these experiences:

- **Child-Adult Reading**—Invite adults to your classroom to read one-on-one with each child. Have the adults read aloud first; then have the children read while the adults assist with any reading difficulties. Invite children to reread the story several times until they can read it fluently.

- **Tape-Assisted Reading**—Children read along in their book as they hear a fluent reader read the book on an audiotape. Use a tape recorder to record yourself or another adult reading the text at a pace of approximately 80 to 100 words per minute. Model intonation and pacing. For the first reading, ask the child to follow along with the tape, pointing to each word in his or her book as the reader reads it. Next, have the child read aloud with the tape until he or she is able to read the book independently (without the support of the tape).

- **Choral Reading**—Read a book to children to model fluent reading. Ask children to follow along in their own book as you read aloud the story again. Invite children to join in when you come to words they know. As you read the book to children a third time, encourage them to read aloud with you. Children should read the book with you a total of three to five times. At that point, they should be able to read the text independently.

- **Partner Reading**—Place children in pairs; more-fluent readers can be paired with less-fluent readers. Have the stronger reader read aloud a page first to provide a model of fluent reading. Then ask the less-fluent reader to read aloud the same text. The stronger reader can assist with word recognition and provide feedback and encouragement to the less-fluent reader. Have the less-fluent reader reread the passage aloud until he or she can read it independently. Partner reading can also be done by pairing children who read at the same level to reread a story that you have previously read to the class. Ask each partner to take turns reading a story to each other several times until they are both able to read it fluently.

- **Reader's Theater**—In Reader's Theater, children rehearse and perform a play for an audience. Provide children with a script that has been derived from a book that is rich in dialogue. Have children play characters who speak lines or a narrator who shares necessary background information. Reader's Theater provides readers with a legitimate reason to reread text and to practice fluency. It also promotes cooperative interaction with peers and makes the reading task appealing.

Comprehension

Regardless of the purpose for reading—enjoyment or gathering information—it cannot be fulfilled if children do not comprehend what they read. Listed below are activities to help children improve their comprehension skills.

Monitoring Comprehension

Before reading a book to the class, tell children that you would like them to raise their hand if they have questions about anything in the story as you read it. As children ask their questions, have the rest of the class give their feedback to help answer any questions that arise. If children are unable to answer a question, you may answer it for them or consult the book, a dictionary, or other reference aid for help. Once all of the questions have been answered, reread the story.

Using Graphic Organizers

After reading aloud a story for the first time, explain to children that good readers are able to identify parts of a story that caught their attention. Many times, good readers can connect these story parts to their own lives. It can remind them of something that happened to them or a feeling they've had. This is called a *text connection*. Reread the story, and ask volunteers to make connections. Give each child a Making Connections reproducible (page 13). Have children list in the left column three events that they liked from the story. In the column on the right, have children list their connection to each event.

Explain to children that good readers are also able to understand how the main character of a story thinks, acts, and feels. Give each child a Character Map reproducible (page 14). Have children write in the center circle the name of one character. Then ask them to write in the remaining circles words that describe the character.

Answering Questions

Read aloud a literature selection. At various places in the reading, stop and ask children questions. Do not ask more than a few questions at each stop since the emphasis should not shift from the primary goal—reading. Ask questions that require children to connect in different ways what they know and what they are reading. See page 15 for a list of sample questions.

Generating Questions

Encourage children to ask questions of themselves and their peers. These questions should be similar in nature and sophistication to the questions you have been asking of them. Challenge children to connect ideas from different sections of the text when they create questions. Encourage them to go beyond the literal fact-finding questions. See page 16 for questions that good readers ask.

Summarizing

After you have read a book several times, ask your class to help you write a summary of what happened. First, have children list everything that happened in the story as you write in chronological order on chart paper what they say. Remind children that summaries should be brief. Make the analogy that a summary is like a tube of toothpaste—you only squeeze out what you need to get the job done and leave the rest in the tube. Decide as a class which parts of the story, while they might be interesting, are not important for understanding the story line. Cross out these parts, and have children rewrite the remaining sentences using transition words such as *first, then, next,* and *last.*

Phonics

Phonics instruction aims to teach children that there are predictable patterns and relationships between letters and spoken sounds. When children understand these patterns and relationships, they recognize known words faster and decode new words more effectively. They read new words better in isolation and in context. The most effective methods of phonics instruction offer direct instruction of specific letter-sound relationships. Phonics instruction must be progressive and specific to be effective, and must provide opportunities for children to use new information in a meaningful context. Because a sequential and complete phonics program is beyond the scope of this book, the activities included in this book are meant to supplement your existing phonics program.

Learning Ring

Cut several sentence strips into small strips of the same length. Place about ten strips in a stack, and hole-punch the top corner of each strip. Use a binder ring to attach the strips together. On the top strip, write a group of letters (e.g., *-igh*) from a letter-sound relationship that children have recently studied. Then write words that include the target letter-sound relationship (e.g., *sigh*, *light*) on the other strips. Place several of these learning rings at a center, divide a small group into pairs, and give each pair of children a ring of words. Have one partner flip through the cards and read each word to the other partner. Then have children switch reader/listener roles.

"Spooling" Words

For this activity, collect several large, empty thread spools. With a permanent marker, write around one of the spools several consonants, blends, or digraphs that are common at the beginning of words. On the next spool, write several vowels, diphthongs, or vowel combinations. On the third spool, write several consonants, blends, or digraphs that are commonly found at the end of words. Place a pencil-top eraser on one end of a dowel (or a round pencil if it's long enough), and slide each spool in order onto the dowel. Place another pencil-top eraser on the other end of the dowel to prevent the spools from coming off. Children can spin the spools to form words. Invite children to make a list of words they can spell using the spools. Extensions of this activity include forming nonsense words and sounding out these words by applying spelling patterns, or adding a spool for either prefixes or suffixes.

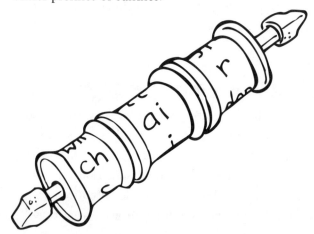

Name _____   Date _____

Making Connections

Write in the left-hand column three events from the story. In the right-hand column, write your connection to each event.

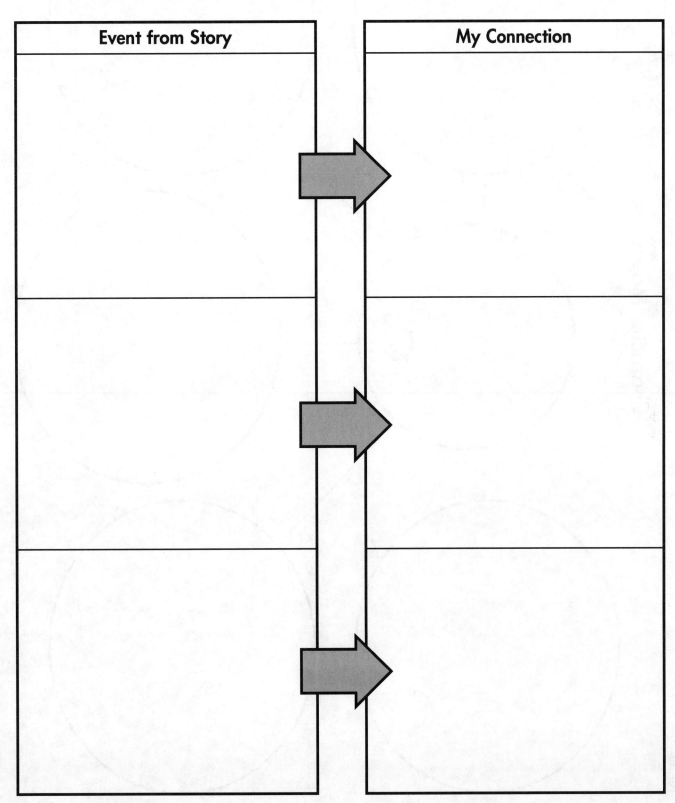

Event from Story	My Connection

Name _____

Date _____

Character Map

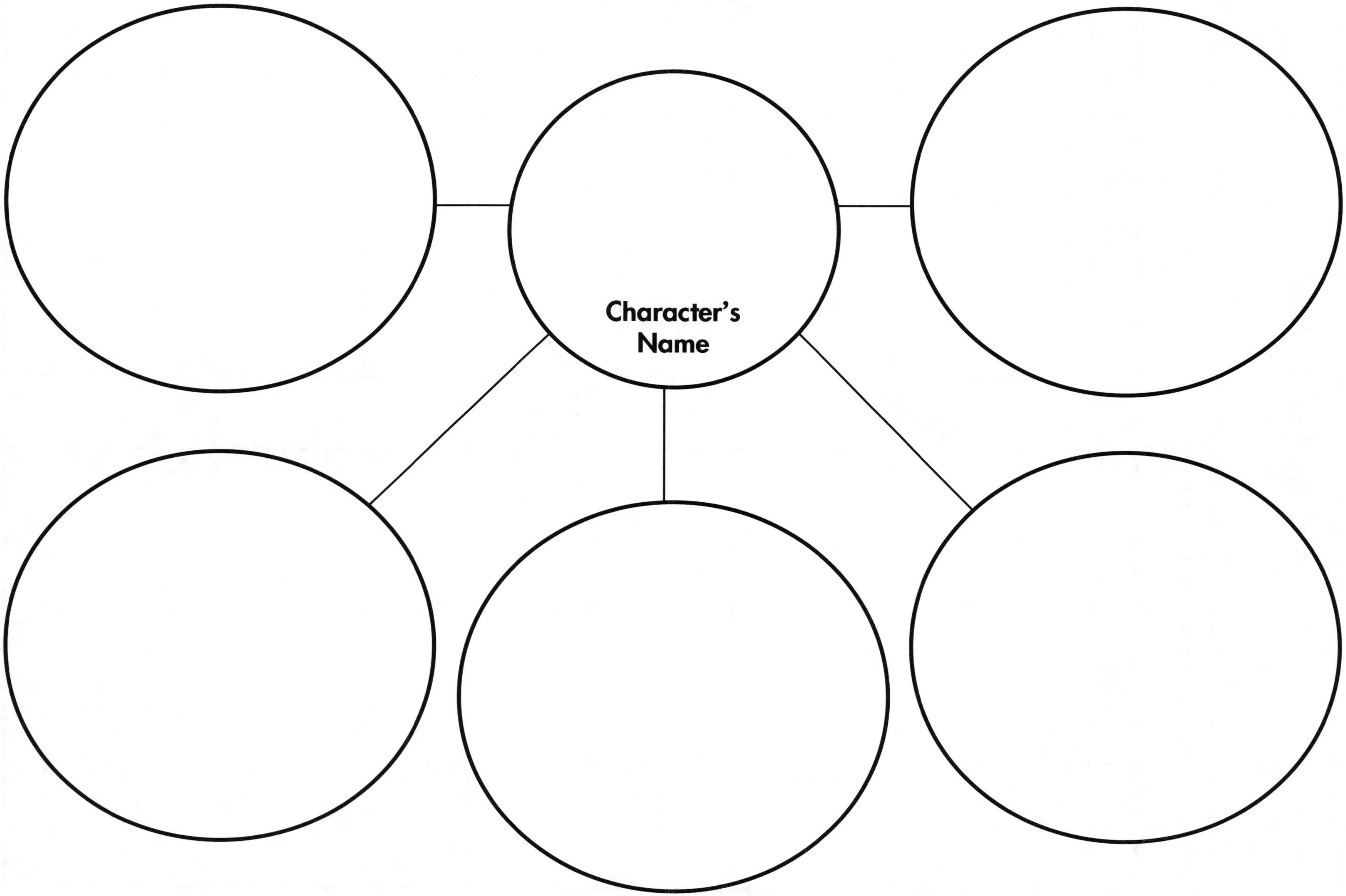

Character's
Name

Questions to Ask Readers

Questions That Connect (i.e., that connect parts of the book to itself or real life)
- How is the character in this book like another character?
- In which part of the story does the character seem happiest?
- Would you be insulted or complimented if someone said you were like the character? Why?
- Do you think the world would be a better place if everyone acted like the character?

Questions That Analyze (i.e., that break the subject into parts and explain each part)
- Who are the characters in the story?
- How is the setting different in the second half of the story?
- How does the character's mood change throughout the story?
- What are some things the characters have in common?
- What problem does the character have?

Questions That Synthesize (i.e., that apply knowledge to what is known and generate new ideas)
- Did the character do what you expected him or her to do? Explain.
- How do you think the character will solve the problem?

Questions That Evaluate (i.e., that give an opinion of the value of the subject)
- How do you think this book compares to the one we read last week?
- Which book do you think is the best one written by this author? Why?
- Do you think this would be a good book to give as a gift? Why or why not?

Questions Good Readers Ask

Questions about the Main Idea
- What is the story about?
- What is the problem?
- How will it be (or was it) solved?
- What do I need to know more about?

Questions about the Events of the Story
- What is going to happen next?
- Do I need to change my prediction?

Questions to Get a Clear Picture in My Mind
- What does this character (or thing) look like?
- What does the setting look like?

Questions to Summarize
- What has happened so far?
- Who did what?

Questions to Clarify
- Would it help to go back and reread that last part?
- Should I ignore and read on? Why?

Alexander and the Terrible, Horrible, No Good, Very Bad Day

by Judith Viorst

(ATHENEUM BOOKS)

In *Alexander and the Terrible, Horrible, No Good, Very Bad Day*, Alexander wakes up to his very worst day as one thing after another goes wrong.

Vocabulary

Using Context Clues

While reading the story to the class, reread the sentence containing the word *scolded*: "*My mom came back with the car and **scolded** me for being muddy and fighting.*" Ask children to guess what the word means based on other information in the sentence. Have children describe the way the mother looks in the illustration. Ask children how they think she is feeling. Have children think of several other words having the same meaning as *scolded*. Invite them to replace *scolded* with the new words and see if the sentence still makes sense. Remind children that words with the same meaning are called *synonyms*.

Fluency

Choral Reading

Read the book to children. Ask them to follow along (in their own book or on an overhead copy of the text) as you read aloud the story again, inviting children to join in when you come to words they know. As you read the book to children a third time, encourage them to read aloud with you if they can. Read the book three to five times with children over several days' time to provide ample fluency practice.

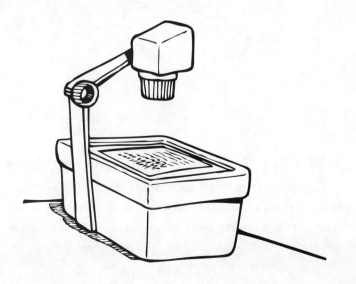

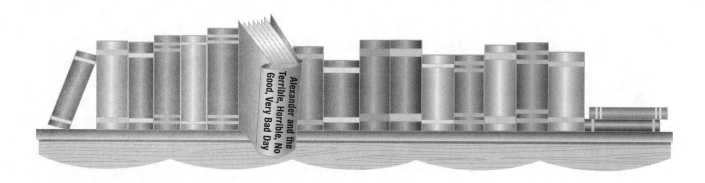

Comprehension

Using Graphic Organizers

After reading aloud the story, ask children if they have ever had a bad day. Have children share different things that happened to them. Ask children if anything that happened in the story to Alexander has happened to them. Ask if the story reminded them of a feeling they've had. Discuss the similarities. Point out that this is called a *text connection*. Give each child a Making Connections reproducible (page 13). In the left-hand column, have children list three events that they could relate to from the story. In the right-hand column, have children list their connection to each event.

Phonics

Contractions

On the board, write the following contractions from the story: *there's, I'll, don't, wasn't, that's, I'm, we're, can't,* and *couldn't.* Discuss the two words that make up each of the contractions, and write them on the board next to the correct contraction. Reinforce this concept through a kinesthetic activity. Have children hold their hands in front of them with their fingers pointed toward each other and their palms facing in. Have children say the two words that make up a contraction, moving each hand as they say a word (each hand representing a separate word). Next, instruct children to move their hands together, interlacing their fingers, as they say the contraction (showing that the contraction is the combination of the two words). Children can pop up their thumbs, one representing an apostrophe and the other the letter or letters removed to make the contraction.

WRITING ACTIVITY

Writing Creatively with Contractions

Reproduce page 19 for each child. Pass out the copies, and put the children in pairs. Have the partners list as many contractions as they can think of and write them in the Contractions box on their papers. Have children switch partners and write down any contractions they might have missed. When children are ready, have them complete the page by writing a story about a bad day. They will need to include at least five contractions in their story.

Writing Creatively with Contractions

Fill in the box below with contractions. Then write a story about a bad day. Include at least five contractions in your story. Circle the contractions in your story with a crayon.

```
┌─────────────────────────────────────────┐
│              Contractions                 │
│                                           │
│                                           │
│                                           │
│                                           │
└─────────────────────────────────────────┘
```

_____
Title

_____

_____

_____

_____

_____

_____

_____

_____

_____

_____

Caps for Sale

by Esphyr Slobodkina
(HarperCollins)

Caps for Sale is the story of a peddler selling caps. He takes a nap with all of the caps on his head and awakes to find that monkeys have taken all of them. The peddler finally finds a way to get back his merchandise.

Vocabulary

Using Word Parts

Explain to children that a prefix is a group of letters found at the beginning of a base word. The prefix changes the meaning of the base word it is attached to. Tell children that the prefix *re-* can mean "again." Next, write the word *fresh* on the board, and look it up in the dictionary. With this definition in mind, ask children to tell you what they think the word *refresh* means. Read aloud from the book the sentence containing the word *refreshed*: "*When he woke up, he was* **refreshed** *and rested.*" Ask children if their definition makes sense within the context of the sentence. Make sure to point out that the letters *re* at the beginning of a word are not always a prefix. The letters are only a prefix if you are able to remove them and a base word still remains. Read the sentence to children again, and ask them to identify a word in which the letters *re* at the beginning do not function as a prefix (i.e., *rested*).

Fluency

Choral Reading

The repeated text in this story is great fluency practice. Read the book to children. Ask them to follow along (in their own book or on an overhead copy of the text) as you read aloud the story again, inviting children to join in when you come to words they know. As you read the book to children a third time, encourage them to read aloud with you if they can. Read the book three to five times with children over several days' time to provide ample fluency practice.

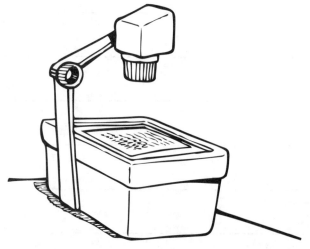

Comprehension

Summarizing

Read the story to children, stopping at the end of each page. Have children summarize each page while you write down the information on chart paper. When you are finished reading aloud the story, have children look over the page-by-page summary. Point out that a summary is a short retelling of a story that includes only the main points. Review the page-by-page summary with children, and have them decide which details are unimportant. Cross out those details to make the summary more concise.

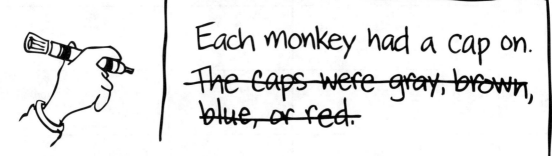

Each monkey had a cap on. ~~The caps were gray, brown, blue, or red.~~

Phonics

The Sound of *qu*

Write *quite* on the board, and read it together with children. Ask children to notice the sound *qu* makes, and have them make the sound in isolation for you. Brainstorm other words beginning with *qu*, and write them on the board. Invite children to look in the dictionary and read other words beginning with this letter combination. These words can include: *quack, quail, quaint, quake, quality, quarrel, quart, quarter, queen, question, quick, quiet, quit, quiver, quiz,* and *quote*. Have children use at least one of these words to write a sentence about the story, and have them underline the word.

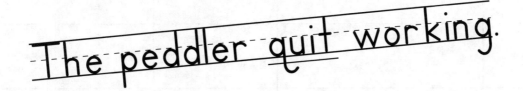

The peddler <u>quit</u> working.

WRITING ACTIVITY

The Prefix *re-*

Reproduce page 22 for each child. Have children write a definition for each word, using the dictionary if necessary.

Name _____   Date _____

The Prefix re-

Write in the space provided the definition of the base word. Then write the new word by adding the prefix **re-** to the base word. Write the definition of the new word. Use a dictionary if needed.

Base Word	Definition	Add Prefix re-	Definition
fresh			
read			
tell			
dial			
name			
deliver			
arrange			
load			
number			
seal			
wash			

Teaching Reading Using Picture Books • 2–3 © 2005 Creative Teaching Press

Where the Wild Things Are

by Maurice Sendak

(HARPERCOLLINS)

In *Where the Wild Things Are*, Max causes mischief, so he is sent to bed without supper. Luckily, a forest grows in his room, and he sails away to an adventure where the wild things are. Homesick, he returns to find his supper waiting for him in his room.

Vocabulary

Using Reference Books

Write the following words on the board: *mischief, private, gnashed, tamed,* and *rumpus*. Divide the class into five groups, and assign each group one of the words. Pass out a copy of the book, a dictionary, and a thesaurus to each group; and tell children that their assignment is to teach their word to the class. The groups find their word in the story, look up the word in the dictionary and thesaurus, and think of ways to help teach the meaning to the rest of the class (e.g., acting out how a wild thing would act before and after it was *tamed*).

Fluency

Child-Adult Reading

To provide children with fluency practice, invite parents to the classroom to read one-on-one with children. Ask the parents to read aloud the story first, and then have children read aloud the story while the parents assist with any reading difficulties. Invite children to reread the story to the parents several times (three to four times if necessary), until they can read it fluently.

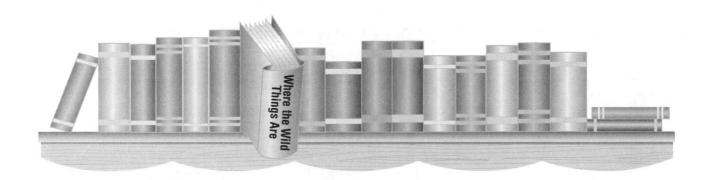

Comprehension

Answering Questions

After reading the story with children, put them in groups of four. Assign a number between 1 and 4 to the members in each group. Read aloud one of the questions below, and give enough time for the groups to quietly discuss the answer. Call out a number between 1 and 4, and have the child with that number in each group give the answer. If there is disagreement about the answer, have children refer to the book for confirmation. Repeat, using the other questions listed below.

1. What did Max wear? (a wolf suit)
2. Why did Max's mom call him a wild thing? (because he was making mischief)
3. What did Max tell his mom? ("I'll eat you up!")
4. What was Max's punishment? (He was sent to bed without supper.)
5. Since a room can't turn into a forest, what do you think really happened? (Answers will vary.)
6. What are three words you think describe the wild things? (Answers will vary.)
7. How did Max tame the wild things? (He said "BE STILL!" and stared into their eyes.)
8. What did they do in the wild rumpus? (Answers will vary based on interpretation of illustrations.)
9. Why did Max give up being king of where the wild things are? (He was lonely and wanted to be where someone loved him best of all.)
10. What happens at the end of the story? (Max is in his room, and supper is waiting for him.)

Phonics

Long and Short *o*

Draw a T-chart on the board or on chart paper. Review with the class the sounds that long and short *o* make. Read each of the following words from the story, and ask children to help you identify the *o* sound in each as a long or short *o*. Write these story words in the appropriate column on the chart: *ocean, boat, off, almost, over, rolled, showed, most, stop, off, lonely, across, so, oh, go, no,* and *hot.*

Long *o*	Short *o*

WRITING ACTIVITY

Writing Creatively with Long and Short *o* Words

Reproduce page 25 for each child. Have children write a story about creating mischief. They should include two short *o* words (circled) and two long *o* words (underlined).

Name _____ Date _____

Writing Creatively with Long and Short o Words

Write a story about creating mischief. Include two **short o** words (circle them) and two **long o** words (underline them).

_____
Title

_____

_____

_____

_____

_____

_____

_____

_____

_____

_____

_____

_____

Teaching Reading Using Picture Books • 2-3 © 2005 Creative Teaching Press

Miss Spider's Tea Party

by David Kirk
(Scholastic)

In *Miss Spider's Tea Party*, Miss Spider is unable to get several bugs to accept her invitation to come to a tea party because they are afraid that she will eat them. Finally, a rain-soaked moth stays and convinces the rest to come and enjoy.

Vocabulary

Repeated Exposure

Read from the book the passage containing the word *descending*: "**Descending** *for a closer look, she danced into the gloomy nook but sadly found those jolly mugs belonged, alas! to rubber bugs.*" Give other examples of how this word could be used in a sentence. Look up the word in the dictionary, or have a child look it up and read it to the class. Invite another child to use it in a sentence. Use the word *descending* at least five times over the course of the day. For example, ask children to line up in *descending* order of heights. Or ask if any child has been on an airplane and if he or she remembers the plane *descending* as it approached the airport. Invite the child to describe what it felt like. Have children draw a picture of something *descending* (e.g., a roller coaster going down a hill).

Fluency

Choral Reading

Introduce the book by reading it to children, modeling fluent reading. Point out the places to pause, to add emphasis, and to change tone. Encourage children to pay attention to how the reader's voice falls into a rhythm with the rhyming text, which helps children learn phrasing. Pass out books or display an overhead copy of the text, and read the text as a group. The story should be reread aloud until children can read it fluently on their own. This may take up to five readings, which can be done at various times during the day or over the course of a week.

Comprehension

Answering Questions

After reading aloud the story multiple times, create a large tic-tac-toe grid on the board or on chart paper. Fill in each space on the grid with a number between 1 and 9. Divide the class into two teams—the x's and the o's. To play the game, ask each team to choose a number between 1 and 9. Read the corresponding question below. If the team answers the question correctly, mark the space with the team's symbol (x or o). The first team to get three x's or o's in a row wins.

1. What kind of chairs did Miss Spider want her friends to sit on? (silken)
2. What kind of beetles crept from the woodwork? (timid)
3. What scared the fireflies away? (the web)
4. What did Miss Spider wave at the bees? (a tea towel)
5. What were the rubber bugs hiding behind? (a broom)
6. What kind of tea did Miss Spider make for the ants? (tea made from hips of roses)
7. Why didn't Miss Spider talk to the butterflies? (she didn't see them)
8. What did Miss Spider do for the moth? (gave him a cloth to dry his wings with)
9. How many insects came to Miss Spider's tea party? (eleven)

1	2	3
4	5	6
7	8	9

Phonics

The Vowel Combination *ea*

Arrange children in pairs. Write these words on the board: *tea, leaves, please, meal, concealed, gleamed, beneath, thread, head, instead, dread, reason, neatly,* and *feast.* Invite children to take turns reading each word with their partner and telling what vowel sound *ea* makes.

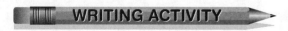

WRITING ACTIVITY

The Sounds of *ea*

Reproduce page 28 for children. Have them complete the page by putting each word on the correct side of the chart according to the sound *ea* makes.

The Sounds of ea

Write each of the words below on the correct side of the chart according to the sound **ea** makes.

meat	death	beak	sweat	tea
each	flea	bread	bead	head

Long e	**Short e**

Write a sentence using a **long e** word:

_____

Write a sentence using a **short e** word:

_____

Teaching Reading Using Picture Books • 2–3 © 2005 Creative Teaching Press

The Little Old Lady Who Was Not Afraid of Anything

by Linda Williams
(HarperCollins)

In *The Little Old Lady Who Was Not Afraid of Anything* a little old lady tries to convince herself that she is not afraid of the different scary objects that chase her on a late night walk. She comes up with a clever idea of what to do with the different objects.

Vocabulary

Extended Instruction

Read aloud from the story the following sentence containing *startled*: "*She was very near her cottage when she was **startled** by a very huge, very orange, very scary pumpkin head.*" Invite one child to look up the definition of the word *startled* in the dictionary and read it to the class. Have children act out being "startled." Invite each child to make up a sentence using *startled* and share it with the class. If desired, arrange children into groups, and have them act out a situation in which they are startled. The rest of the class can guess what is happening.

Fluency

Reader's Theater

After children are familiar with the story, use the book as the script for a Reader's Theater production. Ask children to help you list on the board the characters in the story: the old lady, two shoes, a pair of pants, a shirt, two white gloves, a tall black hat, and a pumpkin head. Add the role of narrator to the list. As a class, change the text into a Reader's Theater script. Put children into groups, and assign a part to each child. Have children rehearse the play until they are comfortable. Provide props (i.e., two shoes, a pair of pants, a shirt, two white gloves, a tall black hat, and a pumpkin head), and have the groups present the play to each other or another class.

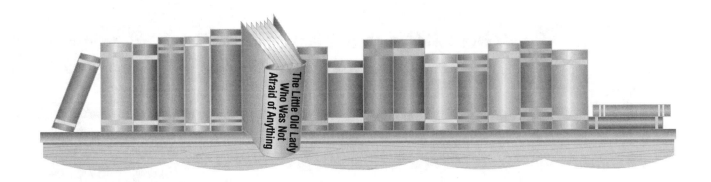

Comprehension

Summarizing

After reading the story, write the words *somebody*, *wanted*, *but*, and *so* on the board. Explain to children that *somebody* is the main character, *wanted* refers to what the main character is trying to do, *but* is the problem the main character runs into, and *so* is how the main character solves the problem. As a class, discuss each element from the story. Arrange children in pairs, and have them write a summary based on these four elements. (You may want to have children fill in the T-chart in the writing activity before writing their summary so they can use the T-chart as a reference.)

Phonics

The Letter *w* and the Digraph *wh*

Write each of the following words on the board, leaving off the *w* or *wh* at the beginning of the word: *windy*, *white*, *went*, *walked*, *way*, *wiggle*, *when*, *was*, *well*, *what*, *we've*, *whispered*, *whistled*, *woke*, and *window*. Write *w* on ten separate sticky notes and *wh* on another five sticky notes. (There are 10 *w* words and 5 *wh* words.) Ask children to help decide if the words begin with *w* or *wh*. Hold the sticky notes up to each word for visual clarification. Have children adhere the correct sticky note to complete each word.

T-chart

Reproduce page 31 for each child. Have children complete the T-chart for the story.

T-chart

Fill in the T-chart with the information from the story. Refer back to the book if needed.

What the Little Old Lady Saw	The Noise It Made

A Turkey for Thanksgiving

by Eve Bunting
(CLARION BOOKS)

In *A Turkey for Thanksgiving*, Mrs. Moose wants to have a real turkey for the first time. She sends Mr. Moose to find one. The invited guests join Mr. Moose as they come upon a frightened turkey. The turkey thinks he's going to be Thanksgiving dinner until he arrives and finally realizes that he's a guest at Thanksgiving dinner.

Vocabulary

Extended Instruction

Write on the board the compound words *Thanksgiving, dinnertime, hillside, riverbank, underbrush,* and *everybody.* Remind children that a compound word is a word containing two smaller words that have separate meanings. Draw a line between the two smaller words in each compound word. Invite children to think of other compound words to add to the list. Reinforce this concept through a kinesthetic activity. Have children hold their hands in front of them with their fingers pointed toward each other and their palms facing in. Have children say the two words that make up the compound word, moving each hand as they say a word (each hand representing a separate word). Next, instruct children to move their hands together, touching their fingers together as they say the compound word (showing that the compound word is formed by putting the two words together).

Fluency

Reader's Theater

After children are familiar with the story, use the book as the script for a Reader's Theater production. Ask children to help you list on the board the characters in the story: Mr. Moose, Mrs. Moose, Rabbit, Mr. Goat, Mrs. Goat, Sheep, Porcupine, and Turkey. Add the role of narrator to the list. As a class, change the text into a Reader's Theater script. (The narrator will read all of the parts in the book that are not within quotations.) Divide the class into groups, and assign a part to each child (a child can play more than one part if necessary.) Have children rehearse the play until they are comfortable, and have the groups present the play to each other or another class.

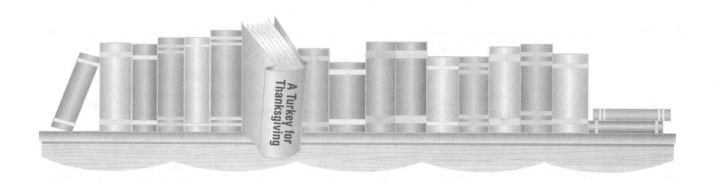

Comprehension

Monitoring Comprehension

This story contains subtle humor that children might not understand at first. While reading aloud the story, pause at different parts of the story to check for understanding. Have children clarify Mrs. Moose's desire to "have a turkey" for Thanksgiving. Ask how many children have had turkey at Thanksgiving. Read until Mr. Moose reaches Porcupine. Clarify the two meanings of "pick me up." Next, discuss why Turkey is so afraid. Discuss the significance of having a chair for Turkey. Lastly, explain the difference between worrying about someone's "taste" and about "how they taste," and the difference between being *on* the table and *at* the table. Reread aloud any section that needs clarification. Review any misleading clues that cause the reader to first believe the Mooses' wanted a turkey to eat.

Phonics

The Sounds of *oo*

On the board, write the words *moose, stood, look, good, too, hooves, wood, booted, hoof, toothy,* and *room*. Have children point out what each word has in common (each word contains a double *o*). Have children say the words out loud and notice the two sounds *oo* makes (i.e., *oo* as in *moose,* and *oo* as in *stood*). Create a T-chart, and have children list the words according to the *oo* sound they make. As a challenge, ask children to look through the book for words that have the same *oo* sound as either *moose* or *stood* but are not spelled with a double *o*.

oo as in m<u>oo</u>se	*oo* as in st<u>oo</u>d
too	look
booted	good
toothy	hooves
room	wood
	hoof

 WRITING ACTIVITY

Vocabulary Practice

Reproduce page 34 for each child. Have children write sentences containing the vocabulary words from the story that are listed on the reproducible.

Vocabulary Practice

Use each of the vocabulary words below in a sentence. If you need help, look in a dictionary, or use clues from the story to understand what each word means.

1 nuzzled: _____

_____

2 bellowed: _____

_____

3 blundered: _____

_____

4 lumbered: _____

_____

5 stammered: _____

_____

6 wobbled: _____

_____

Teaching Reading Using Picture Books • 2–3 © 2005 Creative Teaching Press

Thomas' Snowsuit

by Robert Munsch

(ANNICK PRESS)

In *Thomas' Snowsuit*, Thomas refuses to wear his ugly brown snowsuit. He fights his mother and teacher but in the end puts it on right away when the children outside call for him to come and play.

Vocabulary

Using Reference Books

Read the book aloud, and stop after the first use of the word *enormous* (on the fourth page of text): *"They had an **enormous** fight, and when they were done the teacher was wearing Thomas' snowsuit and Thomas was wearing the teacher's dress."* Ask for volunteers to give you a synonym for the word *enormous*. Pass out thesauruses to the class, and ask children to look up *enormous*. Have each child write one synonym in a sentence and draw a picture to go along with his or her sentence. Display these on a bulletin board titled "Enormous Synonyms."

The <u>gigantic</u> monster scared me.

Fluency

Tape-Assisted Reading

Make a tape recording of yourself or a parent volunteer reading the story. Put a copy of *Thomas' Snowsuit*, the tape, and a tape player in a quiet area for children to use during center time or free time. Instruct children to first listen to the tape and point to each word as they hear it. Next, ask them to replay the tape and read along several times until they can read the book fluently. After children are able to read the book fluently, provide a blank tape and a tape recorder for the children to record themselves reading the text. Invite them to play back their recording and see if they sound like they are speaking naturally.

Monitoring Comprehension

After children are familiar with the book, divide the class into teams. Ask each child (or each team) to come up with a fact about the story and to change one part of it to make it incorrect (e.g., Thomas' snowsuit was *red*). Have the children (or teams) write down their incorrect statement and turn it in to you. Explain that you will choose an incorrect statement and read it to the first team. The team must respond just as Thomas did in the book, by saying *NNNNNO*, and then correct the statement and say it aloud (e.g., *Thomas' snowsuit was* **brown**). Tell children that you will continue to read incorrect statements to the teams in this manner and that a point will be given for each corrected statement. The team with the most points wins.

Past-Tense Verbs with the *-ed* Suffix

Write the following present-tense verbs on the board: *jump, pick, try, look, tie, open, walk, yell, argue, want,* and *move*. Explain to children that if you *do* something, that action is in the present tense (e.g., I *jump* over the stream); but if you already *did* something, that action is in the past tense. Tell children that the suffix *-ed* is added to the end of verbs in the past tense (e.g., Yesterday, I *jumped* over the stream). Use the following format: *Today, I* _____. *Yesterday, I* _____*ed*. Ask children to help write the past-tense form of each verb listed above (i.e., *jumped, picked, tried, looked, tied, opened, walked, yelled, argued, wanted,* and *moved*). As each word is written, draw attention to what happens to the end of the word as the *-ed* ending is added (e.g., the *y* in *try* is changed to *i*; the final *e* in *tie, argue,* and *move* is dropped before *-ed* is added.)

Present- and Past-Tense Verbs

WRITING ACTIVITY

Reproduce page 37 for each child. Have children write the past-tense form of each present-tense verb listed.

Present- and Past-Tense Verbs

Write the past tense for each verb by adding **ed**. Change the ending of the word before adding **ed** if necessary.

Present Tense	**Past Tense**
1 jump	_____
2 pick	_____
3 try	_____
4 look	_____
5 tie	_____
6 open	_____
7 walk	_____
8 yell	_____
9 argue	_____
10 want	_____
11 move	_____

The Hat

by Jan Brett

(G. P. Putnam's Sons)

In *The Hat*, Hedgie the hedgehog gets a woolen stocking stuck on his prickly head. The other farm animals make fun of him, yet in the end, Hedgie gets the last laugh when the other animals put on clothing to stay warm.

Vocabulary

Extended Instruction

Write *magnificent* and *ridiculous* on the board, and define them for children. Read aloud the sentences below. Invite children to decide which word belongs in the blank. Ask the class to create more sentences with blanks to be filled in.

He looked _____ wearing that silly hat. (ridiculous)

It was a _____ play because everyone played their part well. (magnificent)

The great magician's name is Marvin the _____. (magnificent)

It was _____ that I waited 2 hours before they even took my order! (ridiculous)

The pretty flowers in the garden look _____ this year. (magnificent)

It is _____ to think the team could go to the play-offs this year, because they have lost so many games. (ridiculous)

Fluency

Reader's Theater

This story is wonderful as a Reader's Theater. Point out to children how the speakers' tags help the reader know how to read the different text in quotation marks (e.g., the piglets *squealed*, the pony *snorted*, Hedgie *shouted*, Lisa *laughed*). After children are familiar with the story, use the book as the script for a Reader's Theater production. Ask children to help list on the board the characters in the story with speaking parts: Lisa, Hedgie, mother hen, the gander, the barn cat, the farm dog, mama pig, and the pony. Add the role of narrator to the list. As a class, change the text into a Reader's Theater script. (The narrator will read all of the parts in the book that are not within quotations). Divide the class into groups, and assign a part to each child (a child can play more than one part if necessary.) Have children rehearse the play until they are comfortable, and have the groups present the play to each other or another class.

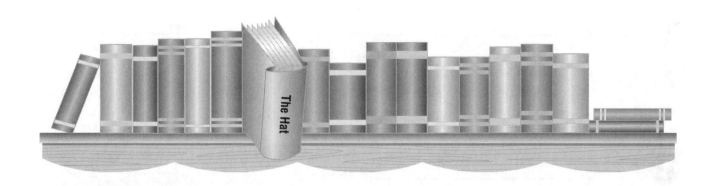

Comprehension

Generating Questions, Answering Questions

Give each child a scrap of paper, and have each child write down a question (with the answer) from the story. Collect the questions, and put children into groups of four. Assign a number between 1 and 4 to the members in each group. Read aloud a question, and give enough time for the groups to quietly discuss the answer. Call out a number between 1 and 4, and have the child with that number in each group give the answer. If there is disagreement about the answer, have the children refer to the book for confirmation.

Phonics

The Letter Combination *-dge*

Write the letter combination *-dge* on the board. Explain to children that these three letters are always found after a vowel and only make one sound—soft *g*. Point out to children that although the letter *d* is silent, it still has an important role. It makes the vowel in front of it say its short sound. Invite children to look through the story for the letter combination *-dge*. Write on the board the words they find (i.e., *Hedgie* and *hedgehog*). Write on the board other examples of words containing these letters (e.g., *pledge, fridge, budge*), and review how these words all have a short vowel followed by the soft *g* sound. Ask children if they can think of other words containing this sound, and add these words to the list on the board. Other words with this letter combination include: *badge, bridge, budget, dodge, edge, fudge, gadget, grudge, hedge, knowledge, ledge, lodge, nudge, porridge, ridge, sludge, trudge,* and *wedge*. Invite each child to choose a *-dge* word and write one or two clues to share with the class so other children may guess the word.

This word has a short i sound and is something to walk on so you don't get wet.

WRITING ACTIVITY

Vocabulary Practice

Reproduce page 40 for each child. Have children complete each sentence with the word *magnificent* or *ridiculous*.

Vocabulary Practice

Fill in each sentence with the word **magnificent** or **ridiculous**.

1 It was a _____ sunset.

2 He did a _____ job as a teacher; all the children loved him.

3 Six hundred dollars was a _____ amount of money to pay for a dress.

4 He looked _____ when he wore his clothes backwards to school.

5 He looked _____ in his pink and purple polka-dotted pants.

6 It is _____ to think a two-year-old can be taught to drive a car.

7 She looked _____ in her prom dress. It was beautiful.

8 When all the flowers bloom, our yard looks _____.

Teaching Reading Using Picture Books • 2–3 © 2005 Creative Teaching Press

I Love You the Purplest

by Barbara M. Joosse
(CHRONICLE BOOKS)

In *I Love You the Purplest*, two boys ask their mother whom she loves more. The mother explains that she loves each of them in a different way.

Vocabulary

Using Word Parts

List the words *lively, juicy, deep, fast, clever, blue*, and *red* on the board. Explain that adding the suffix *-est* to the end of a word makes it the greatest in quality, quantity, or intensity. After the class has an understanding of what this means, write the word with the *-est* suffix next to each word on the board. (Include a discussion about changing *y* to *i*, dropping a final *e*, or adding a consonant before adding *-est*.) Discuss the meaning of each word with the *-est* ending. Have children describe various things that fit into these categories.

As an extension to this activity, you can introduce the suffix *-er*. Explain to children that this suffix means "more." Invite volunteers to say the new form of each word created when the suffix *-er* is added to the original words on the board. Have children decide where these words would fit in the list (e.g., *lively, livelier, liveliest*). Invite children to use the three forms of each word to compare three different things (e.g., The lime was *juicy*, the orange was *juicier*, but the peach was the *juiciest*).

lively – liveliest
juicy – juiciest
deep – deepest
fast – fastest
clever – cleverest
blue – bluest
red – reddest

Fluency

Child-Adult Reading

Invite several adults from school (e.g., the secretary, the principal, the custodian, the cafeteria worker, parents, or classroom aides) to volunteer to help the class with fluency. Pair each child with an adult. Ask the adult to read the story to the child, providing a fluent reading model. The child will then read the book to the adult several times as the adult gives help and support. The child will repeat this process three to four times until his or her reading is fluent.

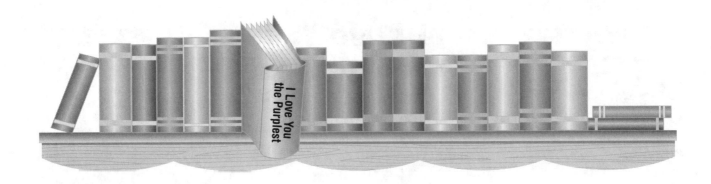

Monitoring Comprehension

Comprehension

This story contains beautiful imagery in its descriptive text. As you read the story to children, stop as needed to clarify meaning. For example, ask the children *What does it mean that the lake slowed its thrashing?* or *What does it mean when it says Max exploded from the cabin?* Stop reading when you come to the part where the mother describes how she loves each of her sons. Have children identify phrases or sentences that are unclear. Have children think about what these could mean and then discuss in pairs what they have come up with. After reading the story, clarify the meaning of the title. Ask children why the color *purple* is in the title but not inside the book.

The /st/ Sound

Phonics

Write *st* on the board, and review with children the sound it makes. As the story is read aloud, ask children to raise their hand if they hear a word with /st/ at the beginning, middle, or end. Answers will include: *sturdy, best, fattest, most, liveliest, juiciest, stepped, strokes, against, stroked, deepest, fastest, stars, hoisting, cleverest, stories, bluest, mist, chest,* and *reddest.*

Descriptive Word Choice

WRITING ACTIVITY

Point out to children that although this book has wonderful illustrations, the author has chosen words and phrases that are so descriptive that the reader can use the words to paint a mental picture. Read the story to children again, but this time, have children close their eyes and picture the story in their head. When you are finished reading, share an example of how the author painted a mental picture for you. For instance, say *Instead of just saying that she loved Max the reddest, she went on to describe things that are red, like "the color of a campfire at the edge of the flame." I could picture that fire in my head and see the color red.* Invite children to share their favorite descriptive words or phrases. Reproduce page 43 for each child. Have children replace the underlined word or phrase with the more descriptive word or phrase from the story.

Descriptive Word Choice

Replace the underlined word or phrase with the more descriptive word or phrase (in the box below) from *I Love You the Purplest*. Rewrite the sentences using the new word or phrase.

slowed its thrashing to a soft, even beat	exploded
stars sprinkled the sky and water turned dark as night	tangle
grew and grew until his cheeks couldn't hold it in	gulped at the air

1 The lake <u>calmed down</u>.

_____

2 Max <u>ran quickly</u> from the cabin.

_____

3 A <u>bunch</u> of worms filled his can.

_____

4 They <u>breathed heavily</u>.

_____

5 They fished until <u>it was dark</u>.

_____

6 The smile on Max's face <u>was big</u>.

_____

The Valentine Bears

by Eve Bunting

(CLARION BOOKS)

In *The Valentine Bears*, Mrs. Bear prepares surprises and tries to wake Mr. Bear from hibernation early to enjoy their first Valentine's Day together. Mr. Bear has a few surprises of his own.

Vocabulary

Repeated Exposure

Write the words *muttered*, *begged*, *shouted*, and *boomed* on the board. Explain to children that good writers often replace the word *said* with other words when using dialogue in their stories. It helps the reader understand how to read the text and see how the characters feel. Read aloud the following sentences from the story:

"Only crazy creatures would be out this early in the year," she **muttered**.

" Just another five weeks," he **begged**.

"Surprise!" Mr. Bear **shouted** and sat straight up.

"You thought I could sleep through just about anything, didn't you?" he **boomed**.

Ask children what each of the boldfaced words means and how the words show what the character is feeling. After children understand all of the words, divide the class into groups of three. Have each group write the words on small pieces of paper and put them in an envelope. Children take turns selecting a piece of paper, reading the word, placing it back in the envelope, and then saying something in that tone of voice. The other children in the group guess which word the speaker had. The first child who guesses correctly goes next. As an extension, children may add to the envelope different words that direct how something should be said.

Fluency

Partner Reading

To provide each child with fluency practice, pair more-fluent readers with less-fluent readers. Have the more-fluent partner read aloud one page from the book to model fluent reading. The less-fluent reader will then read aloud the same page, receiving assistance and support from his or her partner when needed.

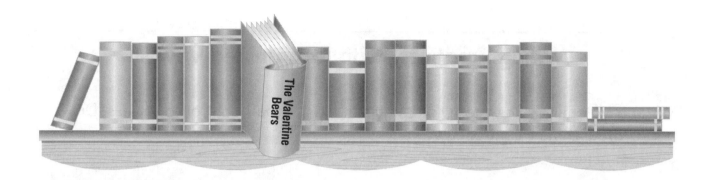

Comprehension

Answering Questions

Divide the class into groups of four. Assign a number between 1 and 4 to the members in each group. Read aloud one of the questions below, and give enough time for each group to quietly discuss the answer. Call out a number between 1 and 4, and have the child with that number in each group give the answer. Teams receive a point for each correct answer. The team with the most points wins.

When did the bears go to sleep? (October 14)

When did Mrs. Bear set the alarm for? (February 14)

Why did Mrs. Bear set the alarm to wake up early? (to spend Valentine's Day with Mr. Bear)

When did Mrs. Bear think Valentine's Day should be celebrated? (summer)

What did Mrs. Bear bury in the fall? (the honeypot)

What did Mrs. Bear call the crunchy dried beetles and bugs? (crispy critters)

How much longer did Mr. Bear say he wanted to sleep? (five weeks)

How was Mrs. Bear going to wake Mr. Bear? (by splashing him with ice-cold water)

What did you expect Mr. Bear would do when Mrs. Bear came inside with the bucket of water? (Answers will vary.)

What did Mr. Bear give Mrs. Bear for Valentine's Day? (chocolate-covered ants)

Phonics

R-controlled Vowels

Write on the board any of the following story words: *bear, secure, winter, her, curled, herself, comfortably, snores, four, later, hardly, remembered, alarm, early, for, first, share, summer, never, years, together, buried, carried, critters, drawer, sharp, creatures, muttered, arms, water, ears, fur, snores, shoulder, harder, turned, another, curled, their, berry, wolverine, deer, surprise, sorry, very, under, here, covered, admired, are, together,* and *were*. Invite your class to read aloud the words together. Explain that each word has an r-controlled vowel in it. Have individual children come to the board and circle the r-controlled vowel. Remind children that there may be more than one r-controlled vowel.

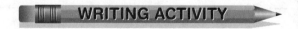
WRITING ACTIVITY

Writing Creatively with R-controlled Vowels

Reproduce page 46 for each child. Have children write a Valentine's Day story containing at least three r-controlled vowels.

Writing Creatively with R-controlled Vowels

Write a Valentine's Day story containing at least three r-controlled vowels. Draw hearts around the r-controlled vowels.

_____

_____

_____

_____

_____

_____

_____

_____

_____

_____

_____

_____

Teaching Reading Using Picture Books • 2–3 © 2005 Creative Teaching Press

Mama, Do You Love Me?

by Barbara M. Joosse
(CHRONICLE BOOKS)

In *Mama, Do You Love Me?* an Inuit girl asks her mother if she will always love the girl no matter what she does.

Vocabulary

Preteaching Vocabulary

Prior to reading the story to the class, show the cover of the book to children. Ask children what they notice about the two characters on the cover (e.g., they are in a boat made of animal skins; both are dressed in heavy coats; both have dark hair and dark skin). Tell children that this story takes place many years ago in northern Alaska, up in the Arctic (show this region on a globe). Explain that the native people there call themselves *Inuit* /IN-oo-it/, although many people refer to them as *Eskimos*. Explain that the Inuit have their own language and that some of their language is used in this book. List on the board the following words from the book: *ermine, lemming, mukluk, ptarmigan,* and *umiak*. Open the back of the book, and show children the glossary of terms from the book. Invite volunteers to look up the meanings of the words. Ask them to read aloud the meanings for the whole class.

Fluency

Partner Reading

This story works well for a partner read since it is the dialogue between two characters—a mother and her daughter. Before assigning partners, remind the children that part of fluency is reading with expression. Fluent readers sound natural when reading aloud, as if they are speaking. Point out to children the rise in voice that's necessary when asking a question. Have children ask questions to practice this voice inflection. Remind children that this story includes many questions. Encourage children to use a natural-sounding rise in voice when reading the questions in the story. Put children in pairs, and have each partner read the lines of one of the characters.

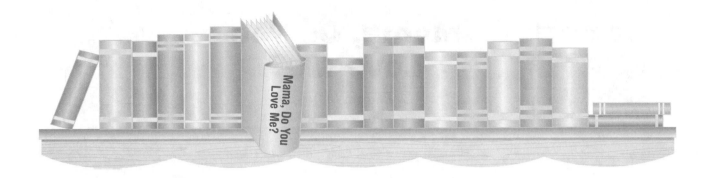

Comprehension

Using Graphic Organizers

After reading aloud the story, ask children if they can remember the new vocabulary words from the story. Write on the board the Inuit words *ermine, lemming, mukluk, ptarmigan,* and *umiak*. Review these words with children, and add any additional words from the story that were new to children or that they haven't heard often. The list could also include animals from the story (i.e., musk-ox, puffin, ravens, polar bear, salmon, walrus, whale, or wolves). Reproduce page 49 for each child. Have children make a vocabulary "quilt" by choosing nine vocabulary words from the board, writing one of the words on each dotted line, and then drawing a picture of each word.

Phonics

Long and Short *e*

Review with children the sounds of long and short *e*. Remind children that words can have either sound. Reproduce on card stock (or other opaque paper) a set of word cards (see page 50) for each child. Instruct children to cut apart the word cards. Have each child read aloud the words and then place the cards in a "Long *e*" or "Short *e*" pile. Read the cards in each pile to check for accuracy. Once children have their cards in the correct piles, invite them to find a partner to play a memory game with. Instruct the pairs to mix their cards together and lay them facedown in an array on the floor or table. Invite children to take turns turning over two cards and seeing if the words have the same vowel sound (i.e., both words are either long *e* or short *e* words). If the words have the same vowel sound, the child keeps the cards and takes another turn. If the child turns over two cards with the same word, the child keeps the cards and takes two more turns. If the words do not have the same vowel sound, the child returns the cards to their places, and the other child takes a turn. The game continues until all of the cards are matched. The child with the most pairs of cards wins.

WRITING ACTIVITY

Long and Short *e*

Reproduce page 51 for each child. Have children write six sentences, using a word with long *e* and a word with short *e* in each sentence.

Name _____ Date _____

Vocabulary Quilt

- - - - - - - - -	- - - - - - - - -	- - - - - - - - -
- - - - - - - - -	- - - - - - - - -	- - - - - - - - -
- - - - - - - - -	- - - - - - - - -	- - - - - - - - -

Long and Short e Word Cards

me	yes	ravens
treasure	eggs	darkness
mittens	be	fell
lemmings	then	slept
meanest	ever	teeth
tent	forever	because

Teaching Reading Using Picture Books • 2–3 © 2005 Creative Teaching Press

Long and Short e

Write six sentences below. In each sentence, use a word with **long e** (circle the word) and a word with **short e** (underline the word).

1 _____

_____

2 _____

_____

3 _____

_____

4 _____

_____

5 _____

_____

6 _____

_____

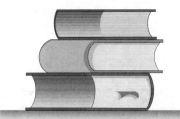

Rumpelstiltskin

by Paul O. Zelinsky

(DUTTON)

Rumpelstiltskin is the tale of a miller's daughter who must spin straw into gold for the king. To do this, she makes a deal with a strange little man. In return, she must give the little man her firstborn child or solve his name riddle.

Preteaching Vocabulary

Before reading the story, divide the class into groups, and give each group one of the following words: *miller, encountered, impress, intrigued, greedier, scarcely, weep, gleaming, vain, piteously, inquiries, posed, thickets,* or *fury.* Ask each group to demonstrate what their word means in three of the following ways: write a sentence using the word, give the dictionary definition, draw a picture of the word's meaning, explain how the word is used in the book, act out the word, or use the word in a skit. Invite each group to share what they have created with the class.

weep
The child started to weep when she lost.

Tape-Assisted Reading

Make a tape recording of *Rumpelstiltskin.* Place the cassette tape and a tape player, along with the book, in a quiet place so children can listen during center time or free time. Have the children listen to the tape several times. During the first tape-assisted reading, invite children to follow along in the book, running their fingers under the words as they read. During each subsequent reading, children will read along with the tape until they are able to read the story fluently.

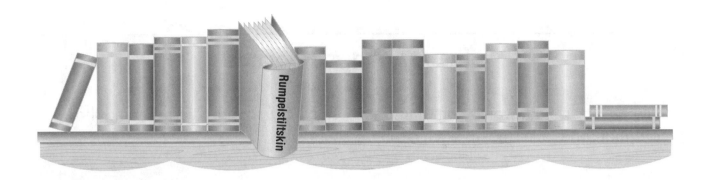

Comprehension

Summarizing

After children are familiar with the story, ask them to write a summary of the story on the bottom half of a piece of drawing paper. Remind children that summaries should be brief. Make the analogy that a summary is like a tube of toothpaste—you only squeeze out what you need to get the job done and leave the rest in the tube. Invite children to choose their favorite part of the summary and then draw a picture of it above the summary. Have them underline that part in their summary.

Phonics

The /s/ and /z/ Sounds

On the board, write the words *necklace, rejoiced, succeed, scarcely, spied, impress, servant, thickets, woods, sunrise, names, queen's, miller's, posed,* and *spools.* Ask children to notice that each word contains one of the following sounds: /s/ as in *said,* or /z/ as in *has.* Have children read the words silently to see if they can determine which sound is in each word. Have children come up to the board, underline the letter (or letters) that makes the sound, and tell which sound the letter makes. Remind the class that some letters make more than just one sound and that different letters can make the same sound.

WRITING ACTIVITY

The /s/ and /z/ Sounds

Reproduce page 54 for each child. Have children fill in each column with words that make the /s/ or /z/ sound. Remind them that more than one letter makes each of these sounds.

The /s/ and /z/ Sounds

Fill in the chart with words containing the /s/ or /z/ sound. Keep in mind that more than one letter makes each of these sounds.

/s/ as in "said"	/z/ as in "has"

Teaching Reading Using Picture Books • 2–3 © 2005 Creative Teaching Press

The Day the Goose Got Loose

by Reeve Lindbergh

(PUFFIN)

In *The Day the Goose Got Loose*, the goose escapes from her pen and causes havoc all over the barnyard. Things settle down once the police arrive.

Vocabulary Preteaching Vocabulary

Prior to reading the story, write the words *riot, sulked, butted, provoked,* and *sergeants* across the board. Read aloud each of the words, and discuss them with children. Ask children if they have heard any of the words used before. Have them share with the class any connections they have to the words. Write these connections underneath the words, and add any pictures that would help clarify the meanings of the words. Be sure children understand each word before reading the book together.

As you read the story for the class the first time, stop at each of the vocabulary words; read them in context, reminding children of their definitions. Reread the story without stopping.

I sulked last night when I had to go to bed.

Fluency Partner Reading

After children have heard *The Day the Goose Got Loose* several times, pair up children of similar reading ability. Read aloud the story one more time, and model how to read with expression. Show children that an exclamation point helps a reader know how to read text. Invite children to take turns reading the text to each other, paying attention to exclamation points. Also point out to children the repeated text: "When the goose got loose . . ." and "The day the goose got loose." When the children read these refrains, have them read chorally. (If there are less-fluent readers in the class, pair each of them with a fluent reader. Have the fluent reader read all of the text except the refrains. Have the fluent reader help the less-fluent reader read the refrains until no help is needed.)

Comprehension

Generating Questions

Before reading aloud the story, do a "picture walk" through the book with the class. Model both literal and inferential questions that could be asked by looking at the illustrations. As children study each illustration, have them share questions they have. Write down the child's name and his or her question on a sticky note, and attach the note to the page where the question was generated. After the story is read aloud, have children discuss which questions were answered and which could not be answered. Discuss possible answers to these unanswered questions or why they can't be answered.

Phonics

Rhyming Words

Remind children that rhyming words can be from the same word family or from different word families. Give an example of each (e.g., *cat—sat, fair—pear*). Copy the rhyming cards on page 57. You will need enough for half of the class size. Place children in pairs, and explain that they will be playing a memory rhyming game. Have them cut out the cards, mix them up, and lay the cards facedown in an array on the floor or table. Invite children to take turns turning over two cards and seeing if the words rhyme. If the words rhyme, the child keeps the cards and takes another turn. If the words do not rhyme, the child returns the cards to their places and the other child takes a turn. The game continues until all cards are matched. The child with the most pairs of cards wins.

WRITING ACTIVITY

Rhyming Words

Reproduce page 58 for each child. Have children write a rhyming word in the blank next to each word. Have them check the box next to the rhyming words that are from different word families (i.e., words for which the rime is not spelled the same).

Rhyming Word Cards

it	quit	mad	had
scared	stared	wild	child
glad	mad	tense	fence
gone	lawn	annoyed	destroyed
sweat	net	why	high
said	head	dream	stream
bear	hair	feet	meat

Rhyming Words

Next to each of the words below, write another word that rhymes with it. Check the box if the rhyming words belong to different word families.

	Different Word Families			Different Word Families
1 bank _____	☐	**9** slim _____	☐
2 flat _____	☐	**10** band _____	☐
3 back _____	☐	**11** chess _____	☐
4 sweat _____	☐	**12** wig _____	☐
5 fine _____	☐	**13** plow _____	☐
6 sound _____	☐	**14** house _____	☐
7 neat _____	☐	**15** lie _____	☐
8 fawn _____	☐	**16** spring _____	☐

Teaching Reading Using Picture Books • 2–3 © 2005 Creative Teaching Press

The Monkey and the Crocodile

by Paul Galdone
(CLARION BOOKS)

In *The Monkey and the Crocodile*, a clever monkey escapes a hungry crocodile who unsuccessfully tries to trick the monkey into becoming his meal.

Vocabulary

Using Word Parts

Write the words *hungry* and *quick* on the board. Discuss with the class what the words mean. Write each word again, next to the original. Add *-er* to the end of each word to create a new word (i.e., change the *y* in *hungry* to an *i*). Explain that adding the suffix *-er* to these words makes a comparison. (In the book, it sets apart the crocodile from the other crocodiles, and the monkey from the crocodiles and other monkeys.) Have children come up with other words ending in *-er*, and add these words to the list on the board. Ask children to draw a picture and write a sentence for each word pair (e.g., Ben was *hungry*, but I was *hungrier*).

Ben was hungry, but I was hungrier.

Fluency

Reader's Theater

After children are familiar with the story, use the book as the script for a Reader's Theater production. Ask children to help you list on the board the characters in the story with speaking parts: the wise old crocodile, the hungry crocodile, and the quick monkey. Add the role of narrator to the list. As a class, change the text into a Reader's Theater script. (The narrator will read all of the parts in the book that are not within quotation marks). Divide the class into groups of four. Have children make costumes and rehearse the play until they are comfortable, and have the groups present the play to each other or another class.

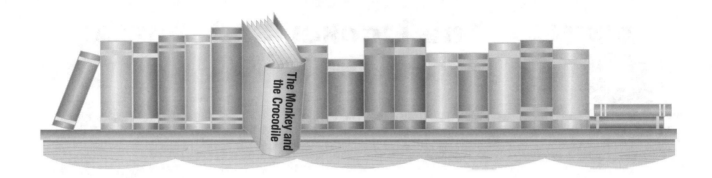

Comprehension

Summarizing

Write on the board the question words *who, where, when, what, why,* and *how.* Review with children what each of these question words means. Have children discuss the main elements of the story that relate to these question words while you write their responses on separate pieces of paper. You may use the following questions as discussion starters:

Who are the main characters of the story? (the monkey and the crocodile)

Where did the monkey want to go? (to the island)

What did the crocodile want? (to eat the monkey)

Why did the crocodile swim under the water? (to drown the monkey so he could eat him)

How did the monkey trick the crocodile the first time? (told the crocodile that his heart was in the tree so they'd have to go back)

How did the crocodile try to trick the monkey? (at night he pretended to be the rock)

After the story elements have been discussed and written down, invite children to work together to organize in chronological order the pieces of paper that have the story elements listed on them. Point out to children that they may not need all of the pieces of paper since a summary is a short retelling of the story that includes only the main points.

Phonics

The Suffix *-ing*

Write on the board the base words *chatter, study, glide, give, turn, take, go, live, jump, watch, wait,* and *sound.* On separate pieces of paper, write (in large handwriting) the letters that are needed to make up the base words (i.e., *c, h, a, t, t, e, r, s, u, d, y, g, l, i, v, n, k, o, j, m, p,* and *w*). Hand these out to children (one letter per child). Also write the letters *i, n,* and *g* on three pieces of paper, and tape the papers together. Give these letters to three other children, and instruct these children that they must stay together to form the suffix *-ing.* Point to one of the base words on the board, and invite children with the letters that make up the word to come to the front of the class and get in order to spell the word. Next, invite the children with *-ing* to add themselves to the end of the base word. Inform children that words ending in *e* require removal of the *e* before adding *-ing.*

 **WRITING ACTIVITY**

Summarizing: Here's the Scoop

Reproduce page 61 for each child. Have children write a summary and list their favorite part of the story.

Name ______________________________ Date ______________

Summarizing: Here's the Scoop

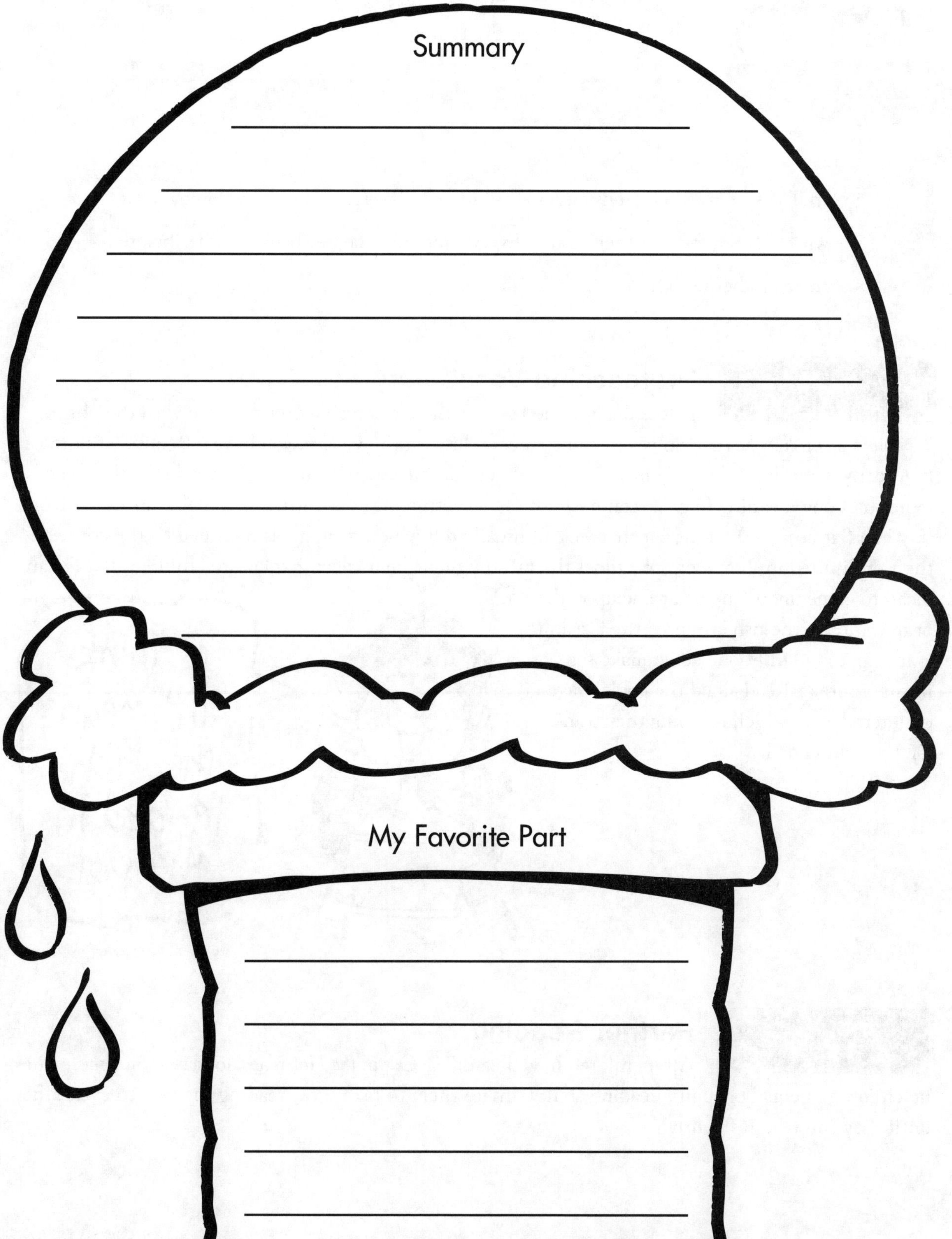
Summary
My Favorite Part

The Cat in the Hat

by Dr. Seuss

(RANDOM HOUSE BOOKS)

In *The Cat in the Hat*, unsupervised siblings are visited on a rainy day by a cat who makes a mess in their house. Everything must be put back in order before their mother returns.

Vocabulary

Preteaching Vocabulary

Before reading the book to the class, read aloud the page with the phrase "*. . . said our fish as he **lit***" (on page 22 or so, depending on the version you have). Remind children that many words have multiple meanings. Invite children to share some words they know that have more than one meaning (e.g., *lie* can mean to say something that is untrue; it can also mean to be or stay in a flat position). Point out that we can usually tell which meaning is intended by the context the word is used in; however, sometimes the meaning may be unclear. Explain to children that *lit* can mean to come upon (the fish came upon the pot) or to criticize (the fish criticized the Cat in the Hat's game)—either one could make sense in this context. Read aloud the book. Have children debate which meaning they think Dr. Seuss intended.

I think "lit" means the fish landed in the pot.

Fluency

Partner Reading

After children have heard *The Cat in the Hat* read aloud several times, pair up children of equal or similar reading ability. Invite them to take turns reading the text to each other until they can read it fluently.

Comprehension

Using Graphic Organizers

Draw the chart below on the board. Have children help you fill in the chart with what happened throughout the book. Reread the book, asking children to help you check the answers.

First . . .		Then . . .		Next . . .		But . . .		So . . .
	→		→		→		→	

Phonics

The Diphthongs *ou* and *ow*

On the board, write the words from the book: *house, out, our,* and *about*. Have children come up to the board, circle the diphthong *ou* in each word, and tell what sound the *ou* makes. Next, write the words from the book: *how, now, down, bow* (verb), and *gown*. Have children come up to the board, circle the *ow* in each word, and tell what sound the *ow* makes. Have children explain what they've discovered (i.e., *ou* and *ow* can have the same sound). Explain that this is not always the case. Invite children to brainstorm other words with this sound and look the words up in the dictionary to see if they are spelled with *ou* or *ow*.

WRITING ACTIVITY

Writing Creatively with *ou* and *ow* Words

Reproduce page 64 for each child. Have children write a story about an unexpected visitor, such as the Cat in the Hat, using the words provided.

Name _____   Date _____

Writing Creatively with ou and ow Words

Write a story about an unexpected visitor. Use at least five of the words below in your story, and underline each of these words.

house	mouse	cloud	shout	sound
flower	clown	crown	down	cow

_____

_____

_____

_____

_____

_____

_____

_____

_____

_____

_____

_____

_____

Teaching Reading Using Picture Books • 2–3 © 2005 Creative Teaching Press

Make Way for Ducklings

by Robert McCloskey

(VIKING)

Make Way for Ducklings is a story about a family of ducks looking for their perfect home. The mother duck causes quite a commotion as she stops traffic to lead her ducklings to their new home.

Vocabulary

Using Context Clues

Explain to children that good readers often use a number of strategies when they come to a word they don't know. One strategy is to look for context clues, which are key words and picture clues that help make sense of an unknown word. First, find the sentences in the story where the words *horrid*, *molt*, *waddle*, and *beckoned* appear. Read the sentences one at a time to the class, omitting the vocabulary words. Ask children if they can think of any word that would fit in the blank so the sentence makes sense. Next, read each of the vocabulary words to the class, and ask children for ideas about the definitions of the words. For each word, reread the sentence where the word appears in the story as well as the previous and following sentences. Invite children to look for clues about the word in the context of the text and illustrations. Remind children that looking for clues can be a great way to figure out words they may not be familiar with.

I think "molt" means feathers fall out.

Fluency

Child-Adult Reading

To provide each child with fluency practice, invite parents to your classroom to read one-on-one with children. Ask the parents to read aloud the story *Make Way for Ducklings*; then have children read aloud the story while the parents assist with any reading difficulties. Invite children to reread the story several times (three to four times if necessary) until they can read it fluently.

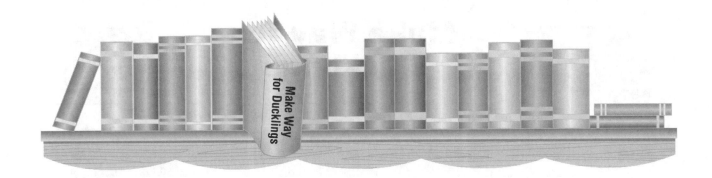

Comprehension

Generating Questions, Answering Questions

Share with children examples of good questions—both literal and inferential (see page 15 for a list of questions). Pair up children, and ask each child to write three questions about the story and trade questions with his or her partner. Instruct children to write the answers for their partner's questions. When they are finished, invite the pairs to read through their questions together to check answers, referring to the book if needed.

Phonics

Long and Short *u*

Review with children the sound of short *u*. Invite children to share a few short *u* words, and then have the class segment these words to isolate the short *u* sound. Next, arrange your class in groups of three to four children. Invite children to list as many words from the story as they can find that contain short *u*. Ask each group to total the number of words found. Have the group with the most words read their list. Write the words on the board, and add any of the following words children may have missed: *but, public, mud, much, enormous, peanuts, ducklings, us, run, rushing, just, lunch, up, tumbled, running, rushed,* and *ducks.* Review the long *u* sound with children, and write on the board a list of words they come up with that contain this sound.

Writing Creatively with Long and Short *u* Words

Reproduce page 67 for each child. Have children write a story about an animal finding a new home. Ask children to include three long *u* words and three short *u* words in their story.

Writing Creatively with Long and Short u Words

Write a story about an animal trying to find a new home. Use three **long u** words (underline them), and use three **short u** words (circle them).

_____
Title

_____

_____

_____

_____

_____

_____

_____

_____

_____

_____

_____

_____

_____

McDuff Saves the Day

by Rosemary Wells

(HYPERION BOOKS FOR CHILDREN)

In *McDuff Saves the Day*, McDuff the dog goes on a picnic with his owners and their child. While McDuff is on guard, ants march off with the family's food. But McDuff befriends a man who invites them to join his picnic.

Vocabulary

Using Reference Books

Write the following words on the board: *marrowbone, invaders, penetrated, introduced, dusk,* and *concertina*. Ask children to look up each word in the dictionary and write the definition down. Arrange children in pairs, and give each pair two copies of the Crossword Puzzle reproducible on page 70. Invite partners to create a crossword puzzle using the words. Partners will make an answer key on one of the copies by writing the words in their place on the puzzle, writing the clues (the words' definitions) below the puzzle, and numbering the word boxes and the clues. The second copy will only have the clues numbered and written in, and the word boxes numbered and outlined. Have the groups switch second copies and complete the puzzles.

				¹i				³c							
				n				o							
				t				o							
		¹m	a	r	r	o	w	b	o	n	e				
				o				c							
				d		²p	e	n	e	t	r	a	t	e	d
				u				r							
				c		²d		t							
				e		u		i							
	³i	n	v	a	d	e	r	s		n					
						k		a							

Fluency

Partner Reading

After children have heard you read *McDuff Saves the Day* several times, pair up children of similar reading ability. Invite them to take turns reading the text to each other until they can read it fluently. After the first reading, encourage children to use the voices of the characters as they read aloud the story. Give the pairs a tape recorder with a blank tape once they can fluently read the story in the characters' voices so they can make a tape recording of the story to put in a listening library.

Comprehension

Using Graphic Organizers

Reproduce and cut apart the Story Map Cards on page 71. Review with children the story elements listed on the cards. Have children give an example of each story element. After reading aloud the book, discuss it with children. Then reread the story to children, and have them place the appropriate Story Map Card on the page where that story element appears. The following are suggested events where the story cards could be inserted:

Introduction — The first page of text is where the characters Lucy, Fred, McDuff the dog, and the baby are introduced. The setting is Lake Ocarina on the Fourth of July.

Main Event One — The family arrives at the lake and gets settled.

Problem — Ants walk away with the picnic food as McDuff stands guard.

Main Event Two — McDuff finds Mr. DiMaggio and eats his meatballs.

Solution — Mr. DiMaggio invites the family to join him to enjoy food and good company.

Ending — The family drives home with McDuff in the front seat.

Phonics

The Letter Combination *-ould*

Write *-ould* on the board, and ask children to say the sound these letters make together. Invite children to look in the book for words that belong to this word family (e.g., *could, wouldn't, would*). Have children think of other words with the same spelling pattern, and write a list on the board.

WRITING ACTIVITY

Summarizing

Reproduce page 72 for each child. Have children use the information from the Story Map Cards to write a summary of *McDuff Saves the Day*. Remind them to only include the main points of the story. Ask children to share their summary with the class.

Name _____   Date _____

Crossword Puzzle

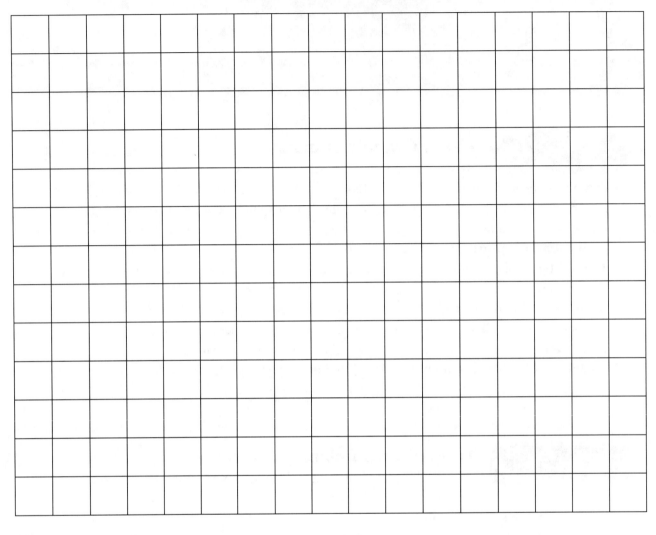

Clues (Definitions):

Across

_____

_____

_____

Down

_____

_____

_____

Teaching Reading Using Picture Books • 2–3 © 2005 Creative Teaching Press

Story Map Cards

Introduction
(Characters and Setting)

Main Event One

Main Event Two

Problem

Solution

Ending

Summarizing

Write a summary of *McDuff Saves the Day*. Remember that a summary is short and only includes the main points of the story. Choose your favorite part of the summary, and draw a picture of it in the box. Then underline that part in your summary.

Teaching Reading Using Picture Books • 2–3 © 2005 Creative Teaching Press

Blueberries for Sal

by Robert McCloskey

(VIKING)

In *Blueberries for Sal*, a young girl named Sal goes with her mother to pick blueberries. She gets separated from her mother and unknowingly starts to follow a mother bear as the baby bear gets separated from its mother and unknowingly follows Sal's mother.

Vocabulary

Using Context Clues

As the story is read aloud, children might not be familiar with the word *hustle* and its variations (i.e., *hustled* and *hustling*). Stop when reading this word, and ask children to look closely at the pictures to see if these can help children determine the meaning of the word. Also encourage children to look for other clues in the sentence or surrounding sentences (e.g., Little Bear *stopped* to eat berries; Little Bear had to *hustle* to *catch up* to his mother; Little Bear's feet were *tired* of hustling). Point out to children that there is a synonym for *hustled* that describes what Sal had to do to catch up to her mother. Can they figure it out? (Sal *hurried*.) For further instruction, take children to an open area, and have them practice "hustling" around.

Tape-Assisted Reading

Make a cassette recording of the story. Place the tape, a tape player, and the book in your book corner. Invite children to practice fluency by listening to the tape and following along in the book by pointing to the words. Next, have them read aloud the book with the tape. Ask children to practice reading the book with the tape several times until they can read the story fluently.

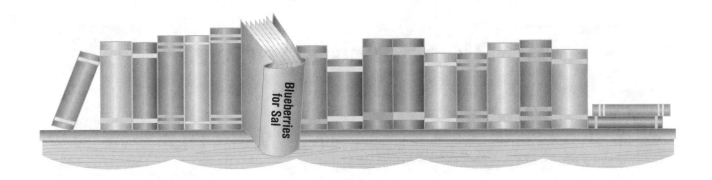

Comprehension

Generating Questions, Answering Questions

Write the question words *who*, *what*, *where*, *when*, *why*, and *how* on the board. Model how to use these words when generating questions about the story. Have children phrase questions about the story using these words at the beginning of the questions. Select children to share their questions with the class, and allow the class to answer the questions. If desired, have a bucket of candy "berries" for children to pick from to reward them for good questions and correct answers.

Phonics

Long and Short *i*

Choose several long *i* and short *i* story words from the list below to write on separate slips of paper (enough so each child can pick one). Place the strips in an envelope, and have each child pick one out. Each child will decide if his or her word has a long *i* or short *i* sound and then confirm it with three other children. As soon as children have identified the correct sound, have them return to their seat. Instruct children to draw a picture using their word and four other words with the same *i* sound (have children list the additional words on their paper). If needed, list all of the words together on the board for children to use as a reference.

Short *i* words: *with, pick, little, tin, in, will, winter, didn't, his, hill, sitting, is, it, children, will, instead, without, partridge, possibly, this, into, mistake, spilled, licking, lips, quickly*

Long *i* words: *behind, tired, right, side, find, I, time, cried, child, like, entire, kind, besides*

WRITING ACTIVITY

Generating Questions

Copy a class set of the Generating Questions reproducible (page 75). Invite children to write questions about the story (using each question word) and then write the answers.

Name _____ Date _____

Generating Questions

Write a question about *Blueberries for Sal* for each question word listed below.
Then answer each question.

Who? _____
_____

Answer: _____

What? _____
_____

Answer: _____

Where? _____
_____

Answer: _____

When? _____
_____

Answer: _____

Why? _____
_____

Answer: _____

How? _____
_____

Answer: _____

Teaching Reading Using Picture Books • 2–3 © 2005 Creative Teaching Press

Swimmy

by Leo Lionni

(ALFRED A. KNOPF BOOKS)

Swimmy is about a small black fish who joins a school of red fish after a large fish eats his family. He teaches the school of fish how to work together to scare off a large fish.

Vocabulary

Repeated Exposure

Read aloud the line from *Swimmy*: "*One bad day a tuna fish, **swift**, fierce and very hungry, came darting through the waves.*" Look up the word *swift* in the dictionary, and read the definition to the class. Ask for volunteers to say a sentence with *swift* in it. Explain to children that when the suffix *-ly* is added to *swift*, the word becomes an adverb that describes how something is done. Throughout the day, ask children to do something *swiftly* (e.g., **Swiftly** *get out your journals; Line up for lunch* **swiftly**). At the end of the day, ask children to make a list of the things they did *swiftly*.

Fluency

Child-Adult Reading

To provide each child with fluency practice, invite parents to your classroom to read one-on-one with children. Ask the parents to read the story to children first, and then have children read the story to parents while the parents assist with any reading difficulties. Invite children to reread the story several times (three to four times if necessary) until they can read it fluently.

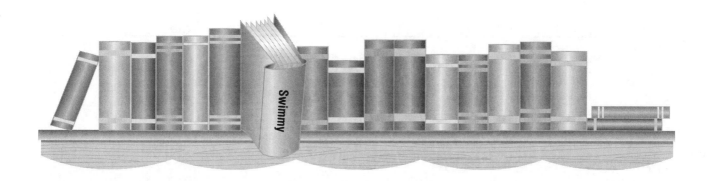

Comprehension

Monitoring Comprehension

As you read the story to the class for the first time, stop each time you read a word or phrase that children may not understand. Ask them to clarify it for you, and then continue to read. Take time to clarify the descriptions of the different creatures Swimmy saw (some of these are listed below). After you have read the book in this manner, reread the story without stopping.

"A happy *school* of little fish . . ."

"He saw a *medusa* made of rainbow jelly . . ."

" . . . strange fish, *pulled by an invisible thread* . . ."

Phonics

The *sw* Blend

Write the following words on the board: *Swimmy, swam, swift, swallowed,* and *swim.* Underline the *sw* in each word, and have children say aloud the blend several times. Invite children to create silly sentences about Swimmy using at least two of the words. (They may use all five if they can.) Invite children to read their sentence aloud, and have the class take a vote on which sentence is the silliest.

Swimmy swiftly swam down
the toilet to freedom.

WRITING ACTIVITY

Tongue Twisters with *s*

Reproduce page 78 for each child. Have children use the *s* words from the story to write and illustrate their own tongue twisters. They may also use a dictionary to look up additional *s* words.

Name _____   Date _____

Tongue Twisters with s

Use the **s** words from the box to make your own tongue twisters. You may use a dictionary to find more **s** words. When you are finished, draw a picture of what is happening in one of your tongue twisters.

school	sea	somewhere	swam	swift
Swimmy	scared	suddenly	saw	see
seaweed	sugar	swaying	shade	swim
strange	said	something	sad	sun

Teaching Reading Using Picture Books • 2–3 © 2005 Creative Teaching Press

 # Literature Selections

The following titles (listed alphabetically by author) are used in this book:

Brett, Jan
The Hat
(G. P. PUTNAM'S SONS)

Bunting, Eve
A Turkey for Thanksgiving
(CLARION BOOKS)

Bunting, Eve
The Valentine Bears
(CLARION BOOKS)

Galdone, Paul
The Monkey and the Crocodile
(CLARION BOOKS)

Joosse, Barbara M.
I Love You the Purplest
(CHRONICLE BOOKS)

Joosse, Barbara M.
Mama, Do You Love Me?
(CHRONICLE BOOKS)

Kirk, David
Miss Spider's Tea Party
(SCHOLASTIC)

Lindbergh, Reeve
The Day the Goose Got Loose
(PUFFIN)

Lionni, Leo
Swimmy
(ALFRED A. KNOPF BOOKS)

McCloskey, Robert
Blueberries for Sal
(VIKING)

McCloskey, Robert
Make Way for Ducklings
(VIKING)

Munsch, Robert
Thomas' Snowsuit
(ANNICK PRESS)

Sendak, Maurice
Where the Wild Things Are
(HARPERCOLLINS)

Seuss, Dr.
The Cat in the Hat
(RANDOM HOUSE BOOKS)

Slobodkina, Esphyr
Caps for Sale
(HARPERCOLLINS)

Viorst, Judith
Alexander and the Terrible, Horrible, No Good, Very Bad Day
(ATHENEUM BOOKS)

Wells, Rosemary
McDuff Saves the Day
(HYPERION BOOKS FOR CHILDREN)

Williams, Linda
The Little Old Lady Who Was Not Afraid of Anything
(HARPERCOLLINS)

Zelinsky, Paul O.
Rumpelstiltskin
(DUTTON)